My Brush with Eternity

My Brush with Eternity

William Rhinehart

This is a true story. The author is a retired bivocational school principal and minister who now lives with his wife in a Covenant Living retirement community in Mercer Island, Washington.

Copies can be ordered online at:
www.lulu.com
www.amazon.com
www.barnesnoble.com
and many other online book retailers

For a free ebook copy, send a request by email to:
rhinehartbb@gmail.com

Also on YouTube

My Brush with Eternity
Copyright © 2020 by William Rhinehart

All rights reserved. No part of this book may be reproduced or transmitted in any form or by any means, electronic or mechanical, including photocopying, recording, or any information storage and retrieval system, except in the case of brief passages embodied in critical reviews or articles, without permission of the author.

Printed in the United States of America.

ISBN: 978-1-7168597-5-5

Cover and interior design by Rick Lindholtz for On the Tracks Media

On the Tracks Media LLC
onthetracksmedia.com

I once experienced two indescribable joys in the same day – the joy of dying and getting a taste of the glory of eternal life – and the joy of breathing again, but with a deep new awareness of God's ever-present wonderful love.

This is my story of that miraculous day.

Bill Rhinehart

"I am the Resurrection, and the Life:

he that believeth in me, though he were dead,

yet shall he live."

John 11:25

The Day I Died | 1

I was feeling so happy that sunny fall day in the 1990s as I drove on a highway in the southeastern United States. It was late on a Thursday afternoon. I had arranged to take Friday off from my job so that I could go to a college football game on Saturday with my two sons. The plan was for me to drive the 90 minutes it takes to get to the college where my younger son was a graduate student, pick him up and start the longer drive together across three states to meet my older son, who was working in the Midwest, on the next day. The three of us would drive together to another state to see the game on Saturday. A lot of traveling, but it was filled with the anticipation of having a lot of fun with my two sons--an opportunity that came all too infrequently now that they were both in their 20s.

The smooth four-lane divided highway with little traffic made it easy to drive close to the 60 mph speed limit. The middle ground between the two sides of the highway was wide and forested so that you couldn't see the traffic heading in the other direction. Occasionally there was a cross road, but no stop signs or traffic lights on the main highway to slow you down. The thought crossed my mind that this beautiful highway could also be dangerous. Just a few days before a man in a pickup truck had driven into the middle ground, hit a large pine tree, and was killed instantly.

Then, suddenly, and with lightning speed, it happened!!! I was riding in the right lane and saw the truck in front of me flash its turn signal for a right turn and start to slow down. After a quick glance to my left and in the rearview mirrors to be sure there were no other cars nearby, I made the fatal decision to ease over to the left lane. In just seconds a disastrous series of events occurred. When I reached the left lane, a loud startling noise began under my car as the tires threw up loose gravel. (I later learned that highway workers putting down fresh gravel on the shoulder of the median had recently stopped work for the day, leaving some of the gravel on the surface of the road instead of taking the time to sweep it clean.)

I slammed on the brakes, but the brakes locked and the cruise control failed to disengage, so I skidded at 60 mph off the road onto the left shoulder, knocking down a highway sign and crashing into the concrete culvert at the intersection of the crossroad. In the split second that I realized that I was going to crash, I stiff-armed the steering wheel trying to break the impact and keep my body in place. I remember thinking, "I'm going to die. This is all wrong. My life isn't supposed to end this way. What about my family?"

Then there was a "BOOM!", the loudest crash I have ever heard. After rapidly turning over four times, the car landed upside down. It was smashed all around, the windshield and rear window were totally shattered, and all the glass in all the side windows was gone. I was no longer sitting upright in the driver's seat. Instead, my body was horizontal, lying on my back on the inside ceiling of the car, facing the front seat which was now over my head. The top of my head was at the open space which previously was the window on the driver's side, and my feet were near what was left of the passenger side window. I was bloody and in great pain. Even though I realized I was probably dying, I said, "Lord, help me," and decided I should try to get out of the car because it could burst into flames any moment. Somehow I knew that the ceiling I was lying on was level with the ground and the window glass was gone. So I unbuckled the seat belt, which was wrapped around me, and, using my arms to grab the window frame and my legs to push, I eased my body out of the car and onto the ground.

    I started yelling, "Help!", and in just seconds I got a response from two men who were racing towards me. In rapid order I learned that these were two truck drivers who saw the accident happen and stopped to help. They could see that I was in a panic state, barely clinging to life. They asked if anyone else was in the car and I said, "No." Then suddenly, unable to breathe any longer, I died.

For I am persuaded, that neither death, nor life,

nor angels, nor principalities, nor powers,

nor things present, nor things to come,

nor height, nor depth, nor any other creature

shall be able to separate us

from the love of God,

which is in Christ Jesus our Lord.

Romans 8:38-39

What It Was Like To Die | 2

Death was instantaneous. My breathing stopped, my heart stopped beating, my eyes closed, and everything went black. There was no fear in the darkness. My soul immediately left my body and all pain was gone. My new weightless spiritual body made a quick, smooth, painless journey through the darkness towards an incredibly beautiful glow. As I approached it, all I felt was wonderful. It was a glorious combination of peace, love, and joy. There wasn't the slightest concern that I was going to be judged and punished for all the sins I had committed on earth. Instead there was an overwhelming feeling of being accepted, forgiven, and loved. The feelings I was experiencing were completely pure and perfect--not like feelings we have on earth, where even the happiest moments are still mixed with the limitations of our minds and bodies. Here we are almost imprisoned in a physical world that inevitably includes pain, sorrow, worry, disappointment, anxiety, sadness, depression, fear--even for the most fortunate of us. Even though I was a firm believer in salvation through Jesus Christ, I had always had a fear of dying. I was sure it would be a very traumatic experience. But when the soul is set free from the restrictions of our minds and bodies, we are surrounded by the love of God, and all is perfectly glorious! It is a spiritual and emotional experience far beyond anything we know on earth.

As I reached the edge of the glowing area, a figure approached me. Since the light was behind this figure and I was still in the dark area, I couldn't see a face, just a silhouette with arms outstretched as if to say, "Stop where you are." I didn't hear a voice like we hear on earth, yet there was clear communication that it wasn't time for me to enter. I was still needed on earth and was being sent back. With lightning speed, I literally zoomed from the spiritual world back to the physical world and landed with a sudden thud back into the body I had left, lying on my back on the ground near my wrecked car. In a split second my heart and lungs started working again.

Back in My Body | 3

I opened my eyes and started taking in the sights and sounds around me. I was still flat on my back on the ground near the wrecked car that fortunately had not burst into flames. I could hear people cheering because I was alive again. A woman bending over me told me that she was an off-duty nurse who saw the accident and stopped to see what she could do to help. When she found me, I was not breathing and had no pulse. She had used CPR to revive me, and because she did not have a stethoscope with her, she was sorry she had to tear open my shirt, saturated with blood, so that she could listen for a heartbeat. A call had been made to the nearest hospital, about 20 miles away, and a helicopter was on the way.

Then a highway patrolman stepped up to me and asked if I felt able to answer some questions so he could complete the accident report. As soon as he finished, he shielded my eyes from the windstorm of dirt created by the helicopter landing nearby. The medics carefully transferred my injured body to a stretcher to load me into the helicopter. One of them then became the pilot while the other stayed with me for the flight to the hospital.

As the medic apologized for repeatedly sticking me with needles in an attempt to attach an IV, I had an amazing discovery. Even though I had not yet been administered any medications, I was experiencing no pain. Before I died, my body was wracked with pain that would be a "20" on a scale of 1 to 10. But my spiritual self, which had just tasted the "unspeakable joy" of the afterlife, was still so strong and so powerful that it completely overruled my mind and my body. I felt like I must be glowing.

At the hospital I was transferred from the helicopter to the emergency room, where they began the process of diagnosing my injuries and notifying my family. After my son and my wife arrived, I was admitted to a hospital room where I stayed for treatment of my injuries for eight days.

While I was in the hospital, an oral surgeon operated on my upper jaw, which was badly damaged. (I couldn't bite and chew at all because of the wobbly upper jaw.) The surgeon had to put my cheek bones back together, using titanium strips and screws. I was put in a brace for my back and neck, because I had several injuries to my spinal column. There was a fracture in C2 in my neck (the vertebra that kills people who are hanged). I had a break in C7 at the top of my back and compression fractures in T5-6 (which made my torso about two inches shorter than previously). I also had a ruptured disk between L3 and L4.

In the months and years that followed I had many medical procedures. There was surgery for a broken nose and deviated septum. Then a turbinectomy to repair my sinuses. Next a microdiskectomy on the herniated disk because it was causing so much sciatic pain in my left leg and foot. I had several rounds of physical therapy, some for the ruptured biceps in my right arm. Subsequent surgeries have included two operations on my right shoulder—rotator cuff and a biceps tenotomy; basal joint surgery on my left thumb; a fusion of four vertebrae, C3 – C6, in my neck; two stents placed in cardiac arteries; and another fusion—this time vertebrae L4, L5, and S1.

There has also been extensive dental work. I now have three permanent bridges—one for twelve upper teeth, two bridges for lower teeth on both sides of my mouth. As a result 23 of my 30 teeth are now made of porcelain. Flossing is quite a project!

One of the worst consequences was learning that the head trauma and dislocated jaw caused me to have sleep apnea. So for many years now I have fought with a CPAP respirator, headgear, and facial mask every night, an experience I wouldn't wish on anyone.

On the other hand, in all these unpleasant, painful experiences, I have known so much peace and serenity. The car wreck was more severe than anything I have ever endured. However, it turned out to be one of the greatest blessings of my life. Now I know that God's loving spirit is with me in all circumstances, as David expressed in Psalm 23: "though I walk through the valley of the shadow of death, I will fear no evil: for Thou are with me."

"And God shall wipe away all tears from their eyes; and there shall be no more death, neither sorrow, nor crying, neither shall there be any more pain."
Revelation 21:4

What Did I Learn By Dying? | 4

There is Life after Death

When my heart stopped beating and my lungs stopped breathing, I didn't cease to exist. I simply passed instantly from one form of life to another. The real me--my soul--was still very much alive. As Jesus promised in John 11:26, "He that liveth and believeth in me shall never die." It was like I had been set free from all the worst parts of me--the physical body with all its pain and suffering, and the parts of my brain that contained all my fears and worries. The "new me" felt incredibly wonderful! I was like a butterfly that had escaped the confinement of the cocoon and had taken flight. As I have looked back and relived that experience, I keep coming to the words "peace, love, and joy," and even these words are so inadequate to describe how glorious the life is that we are going to live forever!

Unfortunately, no human language can adequately express what it was like when I died and experienced a soul set free! But the strong feelings of living in the spiritual world have stayed with me ever since and completely changed the way I look at life and death. As the apostle Paul said, in Romans 8:18, "I reckon that the sufferings of this present time are not worthy to be compared with the glory which shall be revealed in us." In the months immediately following my accident, whenever I reflected upon my experience, I found my thoughts naturally going to poems, songs, and Bible verses about God and eternity and the life to come.

The Transformation is Immediate | 5

It happens so fast! One moment your lungs are breathing, the next they are not. The soul wastes no time getting out of your physical body and beginning eternal life. I did not experience having to sleep for a thousand years, or having to wait for a trumpet call, or spending time in a purgatory waiting for redemption.

I didn't have to lie in a coffin, waiting for a resurrection. It's like there isn't a "death" experience at all, but a continuation of life--just in a new dimension. The "real me" left my temporary earthly body behind and went directly to a great adventure.

It also taught me how quickly this physical life can end. When I started my day, I had no idea that it might very well be my last day on earth. I am more aware of the fact that so many people all around the world start each day thinking that they still have years to live, only to encounter an accident or catastrophe of some sort that suddenly makes it their last day. I think about the hundreds of people who went to work in the Twin Towers on 9/11 with no thought that they would not ever go home. This life we know in our bodies is short, fragile, and can end at any moment. We are always just one heartbeat away from eternity.

"That which is born of the flesh is flesh;
and that which is born of the Spirit is spirit.
Marvel not that I said unto thee,
Ye must be born again."
John 3:6-7

The Soul is a Spirit | 6

When I stopped breathing, I left my pain-wracked body behind. My soul was now a spirit without a physical body. I obviously still had some sort of form, because I "stayed together" as I "flew" through darkness toward the "glow." I still had identity, a sense of "personhood." Although I left my earthly eyes behind, my soul had the vision necessary to see the immense, beautiful glow in front of me, and I could see the spiritual being that stepped out of the light and into the darkness to stop me. My physical mouth and ears were still on planet Earth, but there was a form of communication that allowed this figure to speak to me and allowed me to receive the message--perhaps a type of "brain waves" that didn't require a physical brain. And I experienced very strong feelings--all joyful, glorious, loving, and peaceful--overwhelmingly amazing!

*For a thousand years in Thy sight
are but as yesterday when it is past,
and as a watch in the night.*
Psalm 90:4

Time is Very Different | 7

    One of the most startling revelations I had, as I reflected on my experience in the "afterlife," was how different time is. I don't know exactly how long I was dead. But it must have been at least 10 - 15 minutes-- long enough for a patrolman to arrive and write a report, for a call to the hospital 20 miles away and a helicopter to fly to my location, for a nurse driving by to see the accident scene and park her car and come to my body to administer CPR, and for a group of people to gather to watch, and to hear them cheering when I opened my eyes.

    However long it was that my soul was out of my physical body, it felt like less than a few minutes to me. I definitely experienced that time in eternity is not measured like time on earth. There is a "timelessness" about it, like time isn't a factor at all. It was like I had passed through an invisible wall into a totally different dimension, a world where time really doesn't matter.

    For those of us who have always been such clock-watchers and calendar keepers, it is hard to imagine a life that doesn't have these constraints. It is like there is a freedom just "to be." This time difference might explain things like the creation of our planet, which scientists believe took millions of years the way we measure time, but for God it could have seemed instantaneous. Also, why it is so hard for our time-conscious minds to comprehend eternity, a spiritual world that has always been there and always will be.

Miracles Do Happen | 8

As I reflected on my accident, I absolutely became convinced that several miracles came together that day. A few weeks later, I had the opportunity to go to the junk yard where my car had been towed. What a shock! How could anyone have survived that collision? The car was almost completely crushed, the windshield and rear window shattered, and the glass of the side windows was totally gone. It had collided with the concrete culvert, still going 60 miles per hour because the brakes did nothing to slow it down. On close inspection, I saw that the roof over the driver's seat was the only area that had not been crushed. It was as though something, or someone, had held it up so that my body would not be smashed beyond recognition. It was also miraculous that I had landed in the only position that allowed me to push myself out of the car and onto the ground.

Was it just luck that two truck drivers saw the accident happen and quickly rushed to my aid? Was it just my good fortune that a nurse also saw the wreck and stopped to administer CPR to my dead body? I don't think so. It is harder for me to believe that all of this was coincidental, just a series of natural events, than to believe that something miraculous happened that day, that God acted on my behalf. And to think that God would do this for me is a very humbling experience. As we sing in the hymn, "When I Survey the Wondrous Cross": "Love so amazing, so divine, demands my life, my soul, my all."

If you don't believe in miracles, I recommend that you read Lee Strobel's book, "The Case for Miracles." Hundreds, if not thousands, of wonderful, life-changing events are happening every day all around the world. These miracles are very real and very evident to people who have "eyes to see" and "ears to hear." When you think about it, our whole universe is a miracle of God's doing. Scientists are discovering more and more about the amazing intelligent design that is the result of God's creative work. And this activity on His part is not finished; He continues to act on our behalf all the time. If you don't think that God can possibly be personally involved in all of our lives at the same time, then all I have to say is, "your God is too small." Open your eyes and ears every day and see the miracles taking place all around you and all around the world.

Conclusions and Applications | 9

This Life

Human beings are often described as threefold—body, mind, and spirit. However, after experiencing the reality of life after death, I am so keenly aware that the spirit (or soul) of a person is by far the most important part because it is the one part that lasts forever. My physical body remained on the ground beside my car while my soul passed through an invisible door into the realm of everlasting life.

We human beings are so limited in our vision because all we can see is this world. Of necessity, we devote most of our time and attention to work, physical concerns, and families. The world around us emphasizes physical and material things. Many of us give some of our time to our minds—reading, schooling, and educational media. For most of us, that usually leaves little time for drawing close to God and growing our relationship with Him through worship, Bible study, prayer, uplifting music, and sharing God's love with others. Knowing now that the spirit is the most important aspect of our beings, I realize what a shame it is to waste so much time on physical concerns that are so temporary.

Jesus, who had much to say about this, said: "Lay not up for yourselves treasures upon earth, where moth and rust doth corrupt, and where thieves break through and steal: But lay up for yourselves treasures in heaven, where neither moth nor rust doth corrupt, and where thieves do not break through nor steal: For where your treasure is, there will your heart be also." (Matthew 6:19-21)

God placed us in a beautiful world that is intended to be an enjoyable experience. But we should keep it all in perspective. When we make decisions, we should ask ourselves, "Which of these things will really matter one hundred years from now?"

Preparing for Eternal Life | 10

Throughout history some people have become aware that the main purpose of this life is to prepare for the next one. But some of these efforts have been misguided. Some of the pharaohs of Egypt used their lifetime to have pyramids built to house all the items they wanted to take with them, not realizing that they would have to leave all these earthly things behind no matter how they tried to protect them. Not unlike the pharaohs are the millionaires and billionaires of today who also think the highest purpose in this life is the accumulation of wealth. Others think that fame, or making their mark on history, insures that they will be remembered for centuries to come, a kind of immortality in memoriam.

On the other hand, we have all heard of mystics and cloistered monks who have spent almost all their time in meditation and prayer, totally detached from the world around them. Time spent in this way--worship, Bible study, prayer—is vitally important. However, Jesus calls us to love and care for "our neighbors" as well, to be involved in sharing, giving, and ministering. It is that kind of spirit that led St. Francis of Assisi to leave the confining walls of the monastery to spend his life serving the needs of others, as reflected in his prayer: [1]

> Lord, make me an instrument of Thy peace.
> Where there is hatred, let me sow love
> Where there is injury, pardon
> Where there is doubt, faith
> Where there is despair, hope
> Where there is darkness, light
> Where there is sadness, joy
> O divine Master, grant that I may not so much seek
> To be consoled, as to console
> To be understood, as to understand
> To be loved, as to love
> For it is in giving that we receive
> It is in pardoning that we are pardoned
> It is in dying that we are born to Eternal Life.

How we live does matter, not just now, but forever. As the Bible says, "Seek ye first the Kingdom of God and His righteousness." (Matthew 6:33) In Charles Dickens' book, "A Christmas Carol," Marley's ghost teaches Scrooge, and us, that we forge in this life the kind of life we will experience in eternity. The most important decisions we make in this life are those that affect not our physical bodies, but our souls. Once we realize this, our priorities change. We see the difference between things that really matter because they are of eternal significance, and things that are very temporary.

When God's Spirit teaches us that material things should not be our focus, we begin to look at others with more sympathy, compassion, and empathy. We look for opportunities to show kindness and to share God's love. What God expects of us is not perfection, but trusting in Him to show us what we should do. As the Bible says in

Micah 6:8, "What doth the Lord require of thee, but to do justly, and to love mercy, and to walk humbly with thy God?" And, as Jesus said, in John 15:12, "love one another, as I have loved you." Even Marley's ghost, mentioned above, expresses that "mankind" should have been his business instead of making personal riches his highest priority.

When I died that day in the car accident, I did not feel from God any judgment or condemnation, even though I had not been living a perfect life. As we read in Romans 8:1, "There is therefore now no condemnation to them which are in Christ Jesus." And Isaiah 1:18 says, "though your sins be as scarlet, they shall be as white as snow." All I felt was His forgiving love and acceptance, like the overwhelming love the father of the Prodigal Son showed to him. This warm love allowed me to feel perfect peace and great joy.

You don't have to die to feel God's forgiveness and love. He wants you to experience it now by inviting Him into your heart and life. Jesus said: "Behold I stand at the door, and knock: if any man hear my voice, and open the door, I will come in to him, and will sup with him, and he with me." (Revelation 3:20) You can be part of a "chain reaction" of God's love if you accept His love yourself and share it with others, who will also share it. Then many can experience a loving relationship with God both now and in eternity.

"Bless the Lord, O my soul:
and all that is within me,
bless His Holy Name."
Psalm 103:1

What is a Soul? | 11

Like many people, I had often wondered, "Exactly what is my soul?" From years of religious instruction and listening to sermons, I knew that a soul was something I had. I believed it was a part of me that was going to live forever. But what is this soul like?

There are many words that are used almost synonymously with the word "soul." The Bible and other writings frequently refer to the spirit. Jesus taught that "God is a Spirit, and they that worship Him, must worship Him in spirit." (John 4:24) In other words, when God created us "in his own image" (Genesis 1:26), He gave us a spirit with some characteristics similar to His Holy Spirit, especially the ability to feel and express genuine, sacrificial, eternal Love. Reflecting on my accident, I learned that the soul passes into a spiritual world, a realm invisible to the human eye that is really always there. And even when this spirit/soul is "trapped" for an earthly lifetime in a physical body, it gives us the ability to feel to some extent the glorious peace, love, and joy that we will feel more completely when our souls are set free.

Another word that is often used for the soul is "heart." This, of course, is not the physical muscle in our chests that constantly pumps blood for us 24/7. It is the "heart" that contains our feelings and emotions. It is at the core of our personality and relationships with others. It is used extensively in the Bible. Psalm 51:10 says, "Create in me a clean heart, O God; and renew a right spirit within me." And Jesus, when asked to name the greatest commandment, said "Thou shalt love the Lord thy God with all thy heart." (Matthew 22:37)

Whether we use the word soul, spirit, or heart, we are talking about the part of a person that distinguishes you from a mechanical robot or computer. It gives you a conscience, a demeanor, an aura, an ego, a personhood. It is an ability to be understanding, patient, kind, sympathetic, empathetic, caring, unselfish, and compassionate.

Biologists marvel at the physical bodies God gave us with all our complex cells, tissues, and systems. Neurologists and psychologists continue to learn more about the fantastic brains God gave us with their capability to learn, assimilate, associate, create, and remember. The more we "discover" about our DNA, the more we are just "uncovering" knowledge of things God has known for eons. But the greatest of all God's creations is the soul, because it is the soul that makes everything else work the way it should, and it is only the soul that lasts forever. A crematorium may reduce your body and brain cells to ashes, but it doesn't destroy your soul.

God gave us this soul to enable us to experience Him personally, both now and forever. However, God also gave us the free will to accept or to reject His Son, His laws, and His love. We can choose to be "mean-spirited." We can have hearts that hate. We can be selfish, greedy, egotistical, and unkind. We can value things more than people. We can turn from the teachings of Jesus and even mock those people who do seek to understand and follow Him. The choice is ours.

God wants us to know Him. He seeks out each soul. In His Word we see that God is real, He is our Creator, He loves us, and His commandments are there for our benefit. Since the creation of this world, He has sought our hearts—not by force, but by a covenant of love. He loves us so much that He came to live among us and to save us from certain destruction in life and in death. Our desire on earth should be to live for Him and to share His love with others. As Jesus said, "What shall it profit a man, if he shall gain the whole world, and lose his own soul?" (Mark 8:36) The soul you have when you die is the soul you will have forever. It can be an eternal Hell of separation from God's love, or it can be an eternal Heaven of peace, joy, and love.

Shortly before His crucifixion, Jesus shared these words with His disciples: "Let not your heart be troubled: ye believe in God, believe also in me. In my Father's house are many mansions: if it were not so, I would have told you. I go to prepare a place for you. And if I go and prepare a place for you, I will come again and receive you unto myself; that where I am, there ye may be also." (John 14:1-3).

For by grace are ye saved through faith;

and that not of yourselves:

it is the gift of God.

Ephesians 2:8

The Grace of God | 12

Much of what I have shared may seem like I'm recommending a self-enrichment program, a "create-your-own eternal spirit" regimen. Nothing could be further from the truth. Saving your own soul is not even possible. It is something only God can do. As the Bible says, in John 3:16, "For God so loved the world that He gave His only begotten Son, that whosoever believeth in Him should not perish, but have everlasting life." Those who experience the glory of Heaven are those who are aware of God's love, turn from their sinfulness, and seek His loving Spirit to forgive and guide them.

In John 3: 1-21, we read about a devout Jewish man named Nicodemus who came to see Jesus to learn of Him. In this vitally important conversation, Jesus explains that we receive eternal life by being "born again." Our first birth into this world is a physical birth, which, unfortunately, comes with a soul that is by nature self-centered, seeking personal gratification, often in defiance of the will of God. But the sacrificial love of Jesus Christ gives us the opportunity to be "born again," to have a soul that is in tune with the Spirit of God.

It is so amazing to come to the realization that the great Creator of the universe is also a loving God who cares for each one of us so much that He voluntarily endured the excruciating torture of crucifixion on our behalf. We begin to understand God's "amazing grace" when we acknowledge that He is larger than the universe, yet He knows each of us better than we know ourselves, and He communicates to our individual hearts the great sacrificial love He has for each of us, and He offers us forgiveness for all the pain we have caused Him. Knowing this, how can we turn our backs on Him and refuse to accept His love?

One wonderful aspect of the grace of God is that He wants to be not just someone who allows us to go to Heaven when we die instead of going to Hell, but He also gives us the opportunity to know Him now, in this life, as a companion and friend. Some people find praying to be so difficult because they think of God as someone who is far away, perhaps on a cloud in the sky or even way out in space. You may have heard a person say, "I don't think my prayers get any higher than the ceiling of my room," as if we have to find a way to connect with God long distance. But Jesus taught us that God is not confined to a physical body like the old man pictured by Michelangelo on the ceiling of the Sistine Chapel. As a spirit, God is able to be everywhere at the same time.

What is most amazing is that when we allow Him into our hearts and lives, He is able to make each one of us feel that He is dealing with us directly all the time, that we don't have to "take a number" or "wait in line" to communicate with Him. That is why, when I died in the car accident, I immediately felt a very personal, direct contact with God that immersed me in His love. I was an instant recipient of what Jesus promised in Matthew 25:21, "Enter thou into the joy of thy Lord."

The Peace that Passes Understanding | 13

One of the first things I noticed about being "dead," was that everything was so quiet and peaceful. I had just left a very noisy physical world—the loud crash of my accident, the shouts of people coming to the scene, and my own screams of pain as I cried for help. Then, as my soul suddenly left my body and passed through an invisible wall into the spiritual world of eternity, all the sights and sounds I had just experienced completely disappeared. And in their place was a very restful and peaceful calm.

When you stop to think about it, we live in a world full of noise. Our ears are constantly bombarded by television, radio, traffic sounds, motors, appliances, computers, telephones, etc. Our ears rarely get any rest. Some people even sleep at night in noisy places. But the worst noise in this life may actually not be external sounds that surround us, but the inner noises we experience all the time. Our brain cells are very busy thrusting thoughts at us. And many of these inner communications can be very troubling—worries, fears, physical concerns, anxieties, depression, difficult interpersonal relationships, even thoughts of suicide for some.

The Bible has much to say about the way it should be. Our loving Creator wants so much to set our hearts and minds free of all our fears, worries, and anxieties by trusting completely in Him. As it is written in I Peter 5:7, "Casting all your care upon Him; for He careth for you." He wants to relieve you of all your "inner noises" and replace them with a spirit of peace.

Jesus said, in John 16:33, "These things I have spoken unto you, that in me ye might have peace." And, in John 14:27, "Peace I leave with you, my peace I give unto you. Let not your heart be troubled, neither let it be afraid."

The apostle Paul had much to say about peace in his letters to early Christians: "Therefore being justified by faith, we have peace with God through our Lord Jesus Christ." (Romans 5:1) "Now the God of peace be with you all." (Romans 5:33) "But now in Christ Jesus ye who sometimes were far off are made nigh by the blood of Christ. For He is our peace." (Ephesians 2:13-14) "And the peace of God, which passeth all understanding, shall keep your hearts and minds through Christ Jesus." (Philippians 4:7)

How Joy Differs from Happiness | 14

Probably one of the most universal desires of human beings is happiness. We are very oriented to the importance of being happy. Millions of people every day send someone a wish for a "happy birthday" or a "happy anniversary." When our calendars roll from December to January, billions of people say "Happy New Year." A frequent goodbye is "Have a happy day," or sometimes just "Have a happy."

There are so many ways we try to find happiness. For some people it is sought in love, marriage, and family. Others look for it in their work or recreation. Then there are those who think travel, a vacation, or a cruise will make them happy. Unfortunately, some turn to alcohol, drugs, or other addictive substances in their attempt to find happiness. The sad fact for all of us is that making happiness one of our highest priorities is being nearsighted. It is a form of the philosophy that this earthly life is the only existence we will ever know, so we need to "eat, drink, and be merry." Self-centered happiness is superficial and temporary. When we are happy, it should be a natural byproduct of living a meaningful life.

God wants to give us something much more real and permanent than earthly happiness. The Bible calls this fuller, richer, deeper, and everlasting feeling "joy." Even back in Old Testament days, there was some realization that this joy is an attribute of a right relationship with God. Psalm 43:4 says, "Then will I go unto the altar of God, unto God my exceeding joy." In Isaiah 52:9, we read: "Break forth into joy, for the Lord hath comforted His people." David, repenting of a sin that made him feel distant from God, said, in Psalm 51: "Create in me a clean heart, O God; and renew a right spirit within me. Restore unto me the joy of thy salvation."

When Jesus was preparing His disciples for the fact that He was about to be crucified, part of His message, as shared in chapters 14 – 17 of the Gospel of John, refers to the eternal joy that they were about to experience beginning with His resurrection. In John 16:20 we read, "ye shall weep and lament, and ye shall be sorrowful, but your sorrow shall be turned into joy." And in John 16:22, "ye now have sorrow: but I will see you again, and your heart shall rejoice, and your joy no man taketh from you." In John 15:11, Jesus says to them, "These things have I spoken unto you, that my joy might remain in you, and that your joy might be full."

In the books of the Bible following the gospels, we see the disciples feeling the joy that Jesus promised as they fulfill their commission. In Acts 13:52 we read, "The disciples were filled with joy." Paul writes in Romans 15:13, "Now the God of hope fill you will all joy." In I Thessalonians 1:6 he says, "ye became followers of the Lord, having received the word with joy." The disciple John also shares, in I John 1:4, "these things write we unto you, that your joy may be full." And we find Jude, the half-brother of Jesus who later became an ardent follower, saying in Jude 1:24, "unto Him that is able to keep you from falling, and to present you faultless before the presence of His glory with exceeding joy."

My brief experience in the eternal spiritual world when I left my body behind, confirmed that one of the gifts of God to the soul of a Christian is this indescribably wonderful joy, which, unlike earthly happiness, will never fade or go away. It is everlasting joy!

Jesus saith unto him,
I am the Way, the Truth, and the Life:
no man cometh unto the Father, but by Me.
John 14:6

A Spirit of Discernment | 15

When we become Christians through belief in Jesus Christ as our Lord and Savior and through spiritual rebirth, God gives us this spirit of love, peace, and joy that we have been addressing. But, while we are living in this world, God also gives us a spirit of discernment. The apostle Paul, while discussing spiritual gifts, refers to "discerning of spirits" in I Corinthians 12:10. This ability is necessary because of the powerful presence of evil in our physical world. Whether you refer to evil as Satan, the devil, or a dark force, it is very real and very strong and is constantly devastating the hearts and lives of people. Everyone is subject to the many temptations that surround us every day to disobey God's laws and yield to selfish desires. Many of the great works of literature are about people who are struggling with good and evil, and the ruined lives that result from making the wrong choices.

The Bible has much to say about this. Proverbs 6:18 speaks of a "heart that devises wicked plans." In Jeremiah 17:9, it says, "the heart is deceitful above all things, and desperately wicked." We find Jesus referring to people who are controlled by sinfulness in Mark 7:21-23: "For from within, out of the heart of men, proceed evil thoughts, adulteries, fornications, murders, thefts, covetousness, wickedness, deceit, lasciviousness, an evil eye, blasphemy, pride, foolishness: all these evil things come from within, and defile the man."

Because we live in a world where so much evil is so prevalent, we need God to give us a spirit of discernment. Even though we are taught not to judge others, as Jesus says in Matthew 7:1, "Judge not, that ye be not judged," we are also warned to be careful. Matthew 7:15 cautions, "Beware of false prophets, which come to you in sheep's clothing, but inwardly they are ravening wolves." And in Matthew 7:20, we read, "Wherefore by their fruits ye shall know them." The fifth chapter of Galatians spells out very clearly the differences between people whose lives are controlled by evil and those who allow the Spirit of God to guide them. We are instructed, in Galatians 5:22-25: "But the fruit of the Spirit is love, joy, peace, longsuffering, gentleness, goodness, faith, meekness, temperance. If we live in the Spirit, let us also walk in the Spirit." As Christians, we should be able to discern the hearts of others and if they are believers, have fellowship with them, and if they are not, we naturally yearn to share God's great love for them.

Some Concluding Thoughts | 16

As you have read in these pages, I had an eye-opening, life-changing event. Even though it was so long ago, it is just as vivid to me now as it was then. Dying, experiencing firsthand the eternal love of God, and coming back to earth again has caused me to see life very differently. I now see God's presence and love in everything--people, plants, animals, the earth and sky—even in the darkness. There is genuine meaning, purpose, and happiness in living life with a different perspective, knowing what really makes this life "worth living" and what you <u>can</u> "take with you."

I have struggled for years with the decision whether to share this experience. My hesitation was largely because I do not want to call attention to myself. Rather, it is about God. Kurt Kaiser has written a gospel song called "Pass It On." In this song he says, "That's how it is with God's love, once you've experienced it . . . you want to pass it on." When I had my fatal car wreck, I learned this very emphatically. That is how it is with God's love. Once you've experienced it, you are eager to pass it on. Every day I see people I yearn to tell about God and His love. I can't help but think, "If only you knew Him."

Over the years there have been many others who have had "near death" experiences or brief journeys into an "afterlife." Some of these have related having feelings very similar to mine. I feel very fortunate to have also been so blessed. There is a wonderful assurance knowing from personal experience that God is real, that His Word is true, that He does give us eternal life because He loves us, just as He promises.

I am very much aware that some who read this will be skeptical, especially if they have already convinced themselves that there is no God and no life after death. As Jesus said in Luke 16:31, at the end of the story of the rich man and Lazarus, "If they do not listen to Moses and the Prophets, they will not be convinced even if someone rises from the dead." Jesus himself answered this skepticism by His own resurrection. When He appeared to the doubtful disciple Thomas, Jesus told him to touch His nail-scarred hands and pierced side and "be not faithless, but believing." Thomas answered, "My Lord and my God." Then Jesus replied, "because thou hast seen me, thou hast believed: blessed are they that have not seen, and yet have believed."
(John 20: 27 – 29)

*"Verily, verily, I say unto you,
He that believeth on Me
hath everlasting life."*
John 6:47